W9-CAG-190

Doing and Being Your Best

The Boundaries and Expectations Assets

by Pamela Espeland and Elizabeth Verdick

free spirit
PUBLiSHiNG®

Helping kids
help themselves™
since 1983

Free Spirit, Free Spirit Publishing, and associated logos are trademarks and/or registered trademarks of F Spirit Publishing Inc. A complete listing of our logos and trademarks is available at *www.freespirit.com*.

Library of Congress Cataloging-in-Publication Data
Espeland, Pamela
    Doing and being your best : the boundaries and expectations assets / by Pamela Espeland and Elizabeth Verd'
    p. cm. — (The "Adding assets" series for kids; bk. 3)
    Includes index.
    ISBN 1-57542-171-2
1. Children—Social networks—Juvenile literature. 2. Socialization—Juvenile literature. 3. Child development Juvenile literature. 4. Role models—Juvenile literature. 5. Parental influences—Juvenile literature.
6. Expectation (Psychology) in children—Juvenile literature. I. Verdick, Elizabeth. II. Title.
    HQ784.S56E86 2005
    158.1'083—dc22   2004026'

At the time of this book's publication, all facts and figures cited are the most current available; all telephon numbers, addresses, and Web site URLs are accurate and active; all publications, organizations, Web site and other resources exist as described in this book; and all have been verified as of November 2004. Th authors and Free Spirit Publishing make no warranty or guarantee concerning the information and mat rials given out by organizations or content found at Web sites, and we are not responsible for any change that occur after this book's publication. If you find an error or believe that a resource listed here is not described, please contact Free Spirit Publishing. Parents, teachers, and other adults: We strongly urge yc to monitor children's use of the Internet.

Search Institute℠ and Developmental Assets™ are trademarks of Search Institute.

The original framework of 40 Developmental Assets (for adolescents) and the Developmental Assets Middle Childhood were developed by Search Institute © 1997 and 2004, Minneapolis, MN 1-800-888-78 *www.search-institute.org*. Used under license from Search Institute.

The FACTS! (pages 8, 21, 34, 46, 58, and 71) are from *Coming into Their Own: How Developmental Assets Prom Positive Growth in Middle Childhood* by Peter C. Scales, Arturo Sesma Jr., and Brent Bolstrom (Minneapc Search Institute, 2004).

Illustrated by Chris Sharp
Cover design by Marieka Heinlen
Interior design by Crysten Puszczykowski
Index by Ina Gravitz

10 9 8 7 6 5 4 3 2 1
Printed in the United States of America

Free Spirit Publishing Inc.
217 Fifth Avenue North, Suite 200
Minneapolis, MN 55401-1299
(612) 338-2068
help4kids@freespirit.com
www.freespirit.com

Contents

Introduction

If you knew ways to make your life better, right now and for the future, would you try them?

We're guessing you would, and that's why we wrote this book. It's part of a series of eight books called the **Adding Assets Series for Kids**.

What Are Assets, Anyway?

When we use the word **assets**, we mean good things you need in your life and yourself.

We don't mean houses, cars, property, and jewelry—assets whose value is measured in money. We mean **Developmental Assets** that help you to be and become your best. Things like a close, loving family. A neighborhood where you feel safe. Adults you look up to and respect. And (sorry!) doing your homework.

There are 40 Developmental Assets in all. This book is about adding six of them to your life. They're called the **Boundaries and Expectations Assets** because they're about knowing what's "in bounds" and "out of bounds" for you to do. They're about rules that guide your behavior, and consequences linked to those rules. (Usually, there are good consequences for following rules, and not-so-good consequences for

1

breaking rules.) These assets are also about having people around you—both kids and adults—who encourage you to do and be your best.

The Boundaries and Expectations Assets

Asset Name	What It Means
Family Boundaries	Your family has clear and consistent rules and consequences for your behavior. They keep track of you and know where you are all or most of the time.
School Boundaries	Your school has clear rules and consequences for behavior.
Neighborhood Boundaries	Your neighbors keep an eye on kids in the neighborhood.
Adult Role Models	The adults in your family behave in positive, responsible ways. They set good examples for you to follow. So do other adults you know.
Positive Peer Influence	Your best friends behave in positive, responsible ways. They are a good influence on you.
High Expectations	Your parents and teachers expect you to do your best at school and in other activities.

Other books in the series are about the other 34 assets.* That may seem like a lot, but don't worry. You don't have to add them all at once. You don't have to add them in any particular order. But the sooner you can add them to your life, the better.

Why You Need Assets

An organization called Search Institute surveyed hundreds of thousands of kids and teens across the United States. Their researchers found that some kids have a fairly easy time growing up, while others don't. Some kids get involved in harmful behaviors or dangerous activities, while others don't.

What makes the difference? Developmental Assets! Kids who have them are more likely to do well. Kids who don't have them are less likely to do well.

Maybe you're thinking, "Why should I have to add my own assets? I'm just a kid!" Because kids have the power to make choices in their lives. You can choose to sit back and wait for other people to help you, or you can choose to help yourself. You can also work with other people who care about you and want to help.

Many of the ideas in this book involve working with other people—like your parents, grandparents, aunts, uncles, and other family grown-ups. And your teachers, neighbors, coaches, Scout leaders, and religious leaders. They can all help add assets for you and with you.

If you're curious to know what the other assets are, you can read the whole list on pages 82–83.

It's likely that many of the adults in your life are already helping. In fact, an adult probably gave you this book to read.

How to Use This Book

Start by choosing **one** asset to add. Read the stories at the beginning and end of that chapter. The stories are examples of the assets in everyday life. Then pick **one** idea and try it. See how it goes. After that, try another idea, or move on to another asset.

Don't worry about being perfect or getting it right. Know that by trying, you're doing something great for yourself.

The more assets you add, the better you'll feel about yourself and your future. Soon you won't be a kid anymore. You'll be a teenager. Because you have assets, you'll feel and be a lot more sure of yourself. You'll make better decisions. You'll have a head start on success.

We wish you the very best as you add assets to your life.

Pamela Espeland and Elizabeth Verdick
Minneapolis, MN

A Few Words About Families

Kids today live in many different kinds of families.

Maybe you live with one or both of your parents. Maybe you live with other adult relatives—aunts and uncles, grandparents, grown-up brothers or sisters or cousins.

Maybe you live with a stepparent, foster parent, or guardian. Maybe you live with one of your parents and his or her life partner.

In this series, we use the word **parents** to describe the adults who care for you in your home. We also use **family adults**, **family grown-ups**, and **adults at home**. When you see any of these words, think of your own family, whatever kind it is.

Family Boundaries

What it means: Your family has clear and consistent rules and consequences for your behavior. They keep track of you and know where you are all or most of the time.

BRANDON'S Story

Brandon's mom needs time to straighten out some serious problems in her life. In the past, she's had problems with drinking, and Brandon is pretty sure that's what's happening again. Lately she's been staying away from their apartment for hours, leaving Brandon by himself. Once she was gone way past midnight, and Brandon was pretty scared.

"At least Mom always comes back," Brandon thinks. The thought makes him feel a little better, but not much.

His dad has been out of the picture for a long time, so when things get rough or Mom needs a break, Brandon has to go and stay with relatives. So far, he's stayed with Uncle Jeff, Grandma, and some cousins he barely knows. Just last week, he learned that he'll be going to his Aunt Tanya's in a few days. She lives in another state. "About a million miles away," Brandon mutters to himself.

It's not easy moving from home to home, or learning all the rules in a new place. Brandon keeps wishing that his mom would pull herself together. But so far, all the wishing hasn't gotten him anywhere.

Brandon feels like a ball being juggled by the grown-ups in his life. He never knows exactly where he'll land. The whole thing makes him sad—and angry.

Brandon thinks he doesn't have the *Family Boundaries* asset.

Think about your own life. Does your family have clear and consistent rules for your behavior? (*Consistent* rules are firm and make sense. They don't change all the time or cancel each other out.) Do you know what will happen if you break a rule? Is there usually someone in your family who knows where you are, day and night?

If **YES,** keep reading to learn ways to make this asset even stronger.

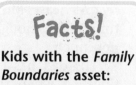

Facts!

Kids with the *Family Boundaries* asset:

✓ do better in school

✓ are more *resilient* (able to bounce back from hard times)

✓ are less likely to do risky or dangerous things

If **NO,** keep reading to learn ways to add this asset to your life.

You can also use these ideas to help add this asset for other people—like your friends, family members, neighbors, and kids at school.

ways to Add This Asset

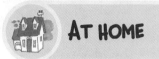

AT HOME

Know the Rules. Most families have rules. Rules are limits on what we can and can't do. Most families also have *privileges* for following rules, and *consequences* for breaking rules. *Example:* One of your family's rules is that you have to be in bed by 9:00 on school nights. If you follow that rule, you get the privilege of staying up until 10:30 on Fridays and Saturdays. If you break that rule, you get the consequence of having to be in bed by 9:00 all week, not just on school nights. Think about the rules, privileges, and consequences in your family that affect you. Do you know what they are?

Make a Contract. If you don't know your family's rules, or you're not clear about some of them, ask your parents if you can work together to make a Family Rules Contract. A Family Rules Contract lists rules, privileges, and consequences in words everyone can understand. Everyone signs it to show they know about the rules. Once your family has a contract, put it where everyone can see it—on the refrigerator, on a bulletin board, or on the back of the door that family members use most often.

A message for you

Sometimes family rules are confusing. Maybe one parent has one set of rules, and the other parent has another set of rules. This can happen in all kinds of families, but it mostly happens when parents divorce and kids go back and forth between two homes. If you think your family rules are confusing, talk with your parents. Ask if they can try to agree on rules that affect you. Or ask if they can agree that some rules will be different sometimes, and that's okay.

Know the Reasons for the Rules. Most rules have reasons. Some rules *keep you safe*—like "Wear your seatbelt" or "Never leave the house without telling an adult first." Some rules *guide your behavior*—like "Bedtime at 9:00 on school nights" or "Use good table manners." Some rules *support your family's values*—like "Always tell the truth" or "Cursing is not allowed." Think of three of your family's rules. What are they good for? Write down at least **one** reason for each rule. *Examples:* "Wearing a seatbelt can save my life if I get in an accident." "If I stay up too late on school nights, I'm tired the next day." "Cursing can be disrespectful."

> **TiP:** Can you think of a rule that doesn't seem to have a reason? (Maybe you don't know what it is, or maybe you disagree with the rule and think it should change.) This is a great topic for a family meeting.

Turn Don'ts into Do's. Maybe you hear a lot of "Don'ts" each day—like "Don't slam the door!" and "Don't hog the remote!" (Maybe you also hear a lot of "You'd better . . ." or "Stop doing. . . .") Rules like this sound negative. Ask your parents if they can put a positive spin on the rules instead. It sounds friendlier when you hear, "Can you shut the door quietly?" or "Please pass the remote." You're a lot more likely to follow a rule if someone asks or reminds you nicely. You might offer to help rewrite some family rules.

TiP: This is another great topic for a family meeting. You could work together turning old "Don'ts" into new "Do's."

Use a Family Calendar. Busy families have a lot to keep track of. A family calendar can help. Ask your mom or dad to get one with lots of writing space. (Or you might offer to make one.) Put it where everyone will see it every day. Everyone starts each week by writing down where and when they need to be and go that week. *Examples:* "Dad: 7:30 PTA." "Mom: Volunteer at library from 1–5." "Eric: Soccer after school." "Shauna: Overnight at Veeta's." You might use a different color of ink or pencil for each family member.

Another message for you

Rules can seem like a big pain. You may think that life without them would be great. You could eat what you want, sleep when you want, play when you want, and do what you want. No one would say, "Do this," or "Don't do that." No one would ask, "Where are you going?" or "Where have you been?" No one would remind you about rules or punish you for breaking them . . . because *no one would care.* Would that really be so great after all?

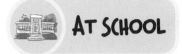 # AT SCHOOL

★ Do you sometimes feel that your parents' rules are unfair? That you don't have any freedom? Think of one or more adults at school you know and respect— teachers, coaches, or the school counselor. Ask them what things were like when they were growing up. What rules did they have to follow? How did they feel about those rules back then? How do they feel about them today?

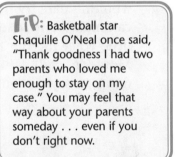

TiP: Basketball star Shaquille O'Neal once said, "Thank goodness I had two parents who loved me enough to stay on my case." You may feel that way about your parents someday . . . even if you don't right now.

 **IN YOUR NEIGHBORHOOD**

★ Family boundaries aren't just for home. They can also guide your behavior when you're out and about. Some kids think they can act however they want when their parents aren't around. They bully other kids, use bad words, and do other things they wouldn't dare try in front of their mom or dad. You can make better choices. At times, you might hear a little voice in your head (one that sounds a lot like Mom or Dad) telling you to think twice before doing or saying something. Listen to that voice.

IN YOUR FAITH COMMUNITY

★ Talk with your religion class or youth group about family boundaries. What does your faith tradition say about how children should behave? About how parents should behave? Are there rules that everyone is supposed to obey? Ask an adult leader to explain these rules so you and your friends understand them.

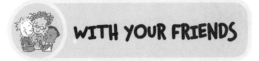

WITH YOUR FRIENDS

★ Sometimes friends pressure each other to try something risky or dangerous. How can you say no without seeming like a scaredy-cat or goody-goody? Use family boundaries as a reason. *Examples:* "If I ever smoke a cigarette, my parents will ground me for life." "I promised my mom I would never ride my skateboard without wearing a helmet."

> **TIP:** If something comes up that your parents haven't covered yet, you can still say something like, "Nah, my dad would get really upset."

Start Adding!

Pick at least ONE idea you've read
here and give it a try. Then think about or
write about what happened. Will you try another
way to make your family boundaries better?

Back to
Brandon's
Story At Aunt Tanya's townhouse, Brandon dumps his clothes out of his duffel bag. Then he starts stuffing them into the guest room dresser, slamming the drawers shut. His aunt sits quietly on the bed watching him. Finally, she asks, "What's up?"

"Nothing," Brandon answers without looking at her.

"Well, 'nothing' doesn't make this much noise," she says. "Let's talk about it."

Brandon plops down next to her. "What's to talk about? It's the same old thing. Me unpacking my stuff in someone else's room. I get dumped on people's doorsteps like a newspaper. I just wanna know something: When will I have a family that cares when I come and go?"

Aunt Tanya puts her arms around him. "I know it's not easy, buddy. You're right about that. But you're wrong about one thing: You do have a family that cares a lot about when you come and go."

"Yeah, right."

"Brandon, I care about you—why do you think you're here? All your aunts and uncles care. Grandma loves you like crazy." Then she adds, "And so does your mom."

When Brandon doesn't answer, she continues. "Look, Brandon, I've got one main rule around here, and it's that we talk about our feelings—even the angry ones—and we put family first."

"That's two rules," Brandon says. Then he looks at Tanya out of the corner of his eyes and smiles slowly.

"Okay, you got me there," his aunt replies. She hands him one of his T-shirts and says, "Come on, I'll help you unpack. Unless you want the totally wrinkled look when you start at school on Monday."

"Thanks, Aunt Tanya . . . I mean, for everything," Brandon says back.

School Boundaries

What it means: Your school has clear rules and consequences for behavior.

Lashondra's Story

It's the big math test everyone has been dreading. Lashondra looks up from a really tough word problem to think. That's when she sees Amy slip a cell phone out of her backpack. Lashondra knows that cell phones aren't allowed in the classroom. Only a few kids have them, including Amy and Brad.

Trying to act natural, Lashondra looks around to where Brad is sitting. He's in the back row, holding something in his lap: a cell phone. Lashondra can't believe it. She's pretty sure that Amy and Brad are text-messaging the test answers back and forth.

"That's cheating!" she thinks. Everyone knows that cheating is against the rules. Plus the school has an honor code that everyone has to sign. When students sign the code, they're promising to be honest and follow the rules.

"Why would Amy and Brad risk getting caught?" Lashondra wonders. "They're two of the best students in our class. All the teachers like them." But that's not all that bothers Lashondra. When some students cheat, it's not fair to others—like her—who study hard, don't cheat, and get the grades they really earn.

Still, Lashondra's not sure what to do. Should she tell the teacher? Should she go up to Amy and Brad later, tell them what she saw, and ask them to turn themselves in? What if they just deny it?

Lashondra decides that, for now, the most important thing is to finish the test. She looks down and tries to forget what she saw.

Lashondra is wondering about the *School Boundaries* asset.

Facts!

Kids with the *School Boundaries* asset:

✔ feel safer at school

✔ like school more

✔ are sent to the principal's office less often

Think about your own life. Does your school have clear rules and consequences for behavior?

If **YES**, keep reading to learn ways to make this asset even stronger.

If **NO**, keep reading to learn ways to add this asset to your life.

You can also use these ideas to help add this asset for other people—like your friends, family members, neighbors, and kids at school.

ways to Add This Asset

AT HOME

Get to Know Your School's Rules. Most schools publish handbooks or handouts about the rules. Look these over with a family adult. Are there any rules you didn't know about? Any you've broken? Any that seem silly or unfair? Are there other rules you wish your school would add? For fun, ask the grown-ups in your family what school rules were like when they were students. Have they changed much since then?

> **TiP:** School handbooks and hand-outs tend to disappear. Do you know where your school rules are? If you can't find them, ask your teacher for another copy. Then keep it where it won't get lost.

Make a "Trouble Tracker." Does your behavior at school get noticed—but not in a good way? Keep a list of times when you get into trouble and why. *Examples:* "Mr. Davis told me twice to stop doodling." "Got caught passing notes." "The principal saw me wearing a T-shirt she didn't like." Try to keep your list for a whole week. At the end of the week, look it over. Are you in trouble a lot? What do you think the reason might be? Are you bored in school? Is it hard for you to listen or sit still? Are you not sure what task you're supposed to be working on? Does it seem that your teacher is picking on you or being too strict? Share your list with a family grown-up. Ask for help.

WANTED: Parent Volunteers!

Parents who volunteer at school are a big help with school rules and boundaries. Some monitor the hallways during times when kids are arriving or leaving. Others volunteer in classrooms. Others come in the afternoon to make sure that students get on the bus safely. The parents get a better sense of what their kids' school is like—and kids get to see their parents in a whole new light. Ask a family adult if he or she has time to volunteer at your school.

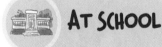

AT SCHOOL

Be a Good Example. Learn and follow your school's rules. If you see someone else breaking a rule, say something. This doesn't make you a goody-goody or a bossy know-it-all. It makes you someone who cares about your school.

TiP: If you don't feel comfortable speaking up to the rule-breaker, go talk to a teacher or your principal. You can choose to stay *anonymous*, or secret. The person you told on doesn't have to know it was you.

Work for Better Boundaries. School is about *rights*, not just rules. You have a right to go to a school where boundaries are clear and people respect them. If your school isn't like this, do something about it. Get together with friends who feel the way you do. Make a list of what you think are your school's biggest problems. (Cheating? Stealing? Fighting? Swearing? Bullying?) Find one or more teachers who will listen and help.

Be a Peer Helper. *Peers* are people from the same age group or place. You and the other kids in your class or grade at school are peers. If your school has a peer-helping program, get involved. (Sometimes these are called peer mediation programs.) Kids in these programs are trained to help other kids by listening to them, offering support and encouragement, and solving problems. Being a peer helper is a great way to help other kids learn about and follow school rules.

Know That Rules Are There for Reasons. If everyone came to school on time, we wouldn't need rules about being tardy. If cheating weren't a problem, we wouldn't need rules about cheating. If no one ever brought a weapon to school, we wouldn't need rules about weapons. Rules exist because some people don't know how to act. And some people choose to act in ways that hurt or bother others. Before you decide to ignore or break a school rule, think about the reason (or reasons) for the rule. What if everyone ignored or broke the rule?

A message for you

Do you often feel afraid or anxious at school? Is it hard for you to learn because other kids are noisy or acting out? Does your teacher spend more time trying to control the class than he or she does on lessons?

Are there some places at your school—like a bathroom or hallway—that you try to avoid? If you answered "Yes" to any of these questions, talk with your parents. Ask them to talk with your teacher or principal. Ask them to spend time at your school, if they can, and see what it's like. They may be able to help. Or they may find another school for you—one where you can learn and feel safe.

 IN YOUR NEIGHBORHOOD

★ If you ride a bus to school, there should be clear rules and consequences for how kids behave on the bus. If kids often act up or cause trouble on the bus, tell a family grown-up. Ask him or her to talk with your school principal or assistant principal.

IN YOUR FAITH COMMUNITY

★ Does your faith community have clear rules and consequences for kids' behavior? You go to church, synagogue, or mosque to learn as well as worship. If you feel that other kids are making it hard for you to learn, talk with your youth leader or religion class teacher. Maybe your faith community needs a "student handbook."

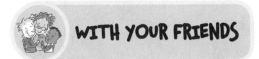 # WITH YOUR FRIENDS

★ Make a pact with your friends at school to learn and follow the rules. Support and encourage each other to do what's right. Help each other to stay out of trouble.

Start Adding!

Pick at least ONE idea you've read here and give it a try. Then think about or write about what happened. Will you try another way to make your school a better place for everyone?

Back to Lashondra's Story   After the bell rings, Lashondra turns in her test. Then she puts her pencil and calculator in her backpack.

"Whoa," says her friend Denise as they leave the classroom together. "*That* was impossible. I am *soooo* glad I studied hard."

"Yeah," Lashondra agrees. "Me, too. But I'm pretty sure not everybody studied as much as we did."

Just then, Amy and Brad meet up outside the lockers. Lashondra overhears Brad saying, "See, it worked!" That's how Lashondra knows her suspicions are right.

For the rest of the day, she thinks about how Amy and Brad broke the rules—and seem to be getting away with it. The more she thinks about it, the more confused she feels.

When she gets home that afternoon, her stepfather, Derek, says, "Hey, you look sort of down. Bad day?"

"Yeah. Can I tell you about something that happened?"

"That's what I'm here for, kiddo," Derek says. "Let's go sit on the couch."

Lashondra curls up beside him and kicks off her shoes. "It was during the math test. Some kids cheated, and I saw it happen. Now I can't decide if I should tell on them or just let it go. I mean, those kids are some of the best students in our class, and they probably just want to keep their grades up."

Derek puts his arm around her and says, "Wow, that *is* a tough one. I'm glad you told me about it. Didn't you all have to sign an honor code at the start of the school year?"

"Yeah," Lashondra sighs, "and that's part of what bothers me. They broke the code, but I saw it happen."

"That's right," Derek agrees. "And if you stay silent, you're breaking the code yourself, because you're not being honest about what you saw."

"But I don't know if I want to set those kids up for getting punished."

"Lashondra, they set *themselves* up. They know there are consequences for breaking rules. Rules are there for a reason, you know?"

"I know."

Lashondra sits quietly for a moment, thinking hard. Then, all at once, she makes up her mind. "I'll talk to the teacher tomorrow," she says. "It won't be easy, but it's the right thing to do."

"That's my girl," Derek says. He gives her a huge hug.

"Hey! You're smooshing me and messing up my hair!" Lashondra says, laughing.

"I can't help it," Derek admits. "You're such a great kid, and I'm just really proud of you!"

Neighborhood Boundaries

What it means: Your neighbors keep an eye on kids in the neighborhood.

Rostam's Story

"Not another block meeting, Mom!" Rostam groans.

"What's all the complaining for?" his mom asks. "You know we do this every two weeks."

"Yeah, but I want to play outside and get on my skateboard. The weather is finally warming up, and I don't want to be stuck at some dumb meeting."

"Come on, Rostam, you know that other kids will be there. Who are you going to play with when all the neighbors are over at Mr. Lee's, anyway? We've got important things to talk about tonight, including the new speed bump we want." Then she smiles and adds, "Plus we're planning the ice-cream social."

Rostam remembers what fun the ice-cream social was last year. He had promised everyone he would make a sundae with everything on it—and he meant

everything, including gumballs and even a couple of crackers off his mom's plate to make everyone laugh.

But now, he goes over to the window and thinks about what a nice night it is for skateboarding. "I'm not going," he says flatly.

His mom gives him "the look": a familiar raised-eyebrow scowl that tells Rostam his mom has reached her limit. "Well, how do you think Mr. Lee is going to like it if you don't show up?"

Rostam rolls his eyes. He's annoyed, but deep down, he really likes Mr. Lee and doesn't want to disappoint him.

Sometimes Rostam has mixed feelings about the *Neighborhood Boundaries* asset.

Think about your own life. Do you feel that your neighbors keep an eye on you and other kids in the neighborhood? Does it seem that your neighbors really care about each other and don't just look the other way?

If **YES**, keep reading to learn ways to make this asset even stronger.

If **NO**, keep reading to learn ways to add this asset to your life.

Facts!

Kids with the *Neighborhood Boundaries* **asset:**

✔ score higher on achievement tests

✔ have fewer behavior problems

✔ are less likely to make friends who are troublemakers

You can also use these ideas to help add this asset for other people—like your friends, family members, neighbors, and kids at school.

ways to Add This Asset

AT HOME

Be a Good Neighbor. What makes someone a good neighbor? Being friendly, kind, and respectful. This is something you can do. *Examples:* Give your neighbors a wave and a smile as you pass by. Don't throw litter in their yards. If you walk your dog around the neighborhood, pick up the you-know-what. Give someone a compliment now and then: "Love the tulips, Mr. Lorenzo!" Or offer to lend a hand: "Can I help you wash your car, Ms. Washington?"

Know When It's Okay to Share. If you're lucky enough to have backyard swings and other outdoor play equipment, like bikes or a basketball hoop, the kids in your neighborhood may want to give your stuff a try. Does your family have rules about sharing or not sharing? Some families welcome kids from all over the neighborhood to hang out in their yard, in their driveway, or on their porch. Other families don't feel comfortable doing that. What are the rules for your home and yard? What should you do if other kids don't follow the rules? And what about times when *you* want to use things that belong to other kids? Talk to a family adult who can help you figure out how to handle times like these.

> **TiP:** If your place is a hang-out for lots of kids, at least one of your parents should be at home when other kids are there. And if you're going to be at a friend's house, at least one of his or her parents should be at home.

Look Out for Younger Children. As one of the older (and wiser) kids on your block, you can help make sure the younger ones are following the rules. Are they watching out for traffic—or running out into the street? Are they sharing toys—or fighting over them? Are they hogging the slide—or taking turns? Sometimes, you can be the one to show them how to do the right thing. Notice if they're throwing sand at each other, or if they stray too far from their parents or baby-sitters. If a child is in any kind of danger, tell a parent or another grown-up right away.

A message for you

Suppose that an adult neighbor is telling you what to do or not do. Do you have to listen? That depends. If this is a grown-up you and your parents know and trust, he or she is probably watching out for you. But if you don't know this particular neighbor and you have doubts about what you're hearing, talk to your parents or another family adult. Explain what's happening and ask for advice.

 ## AT SCHOOL

⭐ Is your school in a neighborhood? If it is, act like you live there. Be respectful of the neighbors' yards when you walk to and from school. Don't trample people's flowers or throw litter on the ground. Even if your school is on many acres of land in a suburb or out in the country, you can still be on your best behavior when you're on school grounds or nearby.

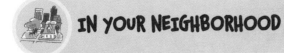

IN YOUR NEIGHBORHOOD

Join the Neighborhood Watch.
Keep your eyes and ears open for things that are going wrong (or right) in your neighborhood. Let your parents know what you've seen and heard. *Examples:* "Some kids down the street were tipping over garbage cans." "Someone finally cleaned up the broken glass by the park."

Help to Create Neighborhood Boundaries. Tell your parents that you want your neighborhood to be safer, cleaner, and friendlier. Ask if they would be willing to talk with other adults in the neighborhood. Maybe they could host a block party, or building party, or front-yard party. Adults and kids could talk together about neighborhood boundaries. Everyone could agree on a few to start with.

4 Basic Neighborhood Boundaries

These would make good boundaries for any neighborhood:

1. We agree to watch out for each other and help each other.

2. We agree to report suspicious activity. Kids will tell their parents or other family adults. Grown-ups will call the police.

3. We agree to respect people and property.

4. We agree to be good role models for each other.

IN YOUR FAITH COMMUNITY

★ Are there adults in your faith community who watch out for kids? Think of the grown-ups who teach religion classes, lead the youth group, and help out in the nursery. Think of those who might say *"Shhhhh"* if you talk during prayers or services. These people are helping to set boundaries for your behavior. What are you learning from them?

WITH YOUR FRIENDS

★ When you're at a friend's home, try to be on your best behavior. Respect the rules even if they're different from what you're used to. If you don't know the rules, ask the grown-ups about them. *Examples:* "Is it okay if I use the phone?" "Are we allowed to play softball out front?" "Will the neighbors care if we ride bikes on the sidewalk, or can we only bike in the street?"

Start Adding!

Pick at least ONE idea you've read here and give it a try. Then think about or write about what happened. Will you try another way to make your neighborhood a better place for everyone who lives there?

Back to Rostam's Story

"Mom, can't you just make something up so I don't have to go to the meeting? Tell Mr. Lee I'm sick," Rostam says.

"Oh no, you don't," his mom warns.

"I'm not going to lie. Besides, all Mr. Lee has to do is look out his window and see you on your skateboard—then what's he going to think?"

Rostam wonders what it would be like to live in a neighborhood where you'd have a little peace, and maybe even some privacy once in a while. The adults on his block are always getting in his face, asking him questions about school and stuff. Just the other day, Mrs. Hinz called out her window, "Rostam! You're too far out in the street—get back on the sidewalk with that skateboard before you get yourself hit by a car!"

"And now another block meeting," Rostam thinks. "That means listening to the neighbors talk about rules, and curfews, and who's doing what. *Bor-iiiing!*"

Then he sees some of the neighbors making their way over to Mr. Lee's, laughing and talking. Some of them are carrying food containers, and Rostam wonders what's inside. A couple of his friends are in the group—and everyone looks like they're having a pretty good time.

Rostam starts having second thoughts. "Maybe it's not so bad going to a neighborhood thing once in a while. I guess I'd rather have neighbors who care about me than ones who don't even know who I am."

"Okay, you win, Mom," Rostam says. His mom smiles and says she's proud of him. Rostam runs out the door and calls to his friends, "Hey, guys! Wait up!"

Adult Role Models

What it means: The adults in your family behave in positive, responsible ways. They set good examples for you to follow. So do other adults you know.

Tameka's Story

"Look at these two lovely, brilliant young women," says Tameka's dad, reaching for his digital camera.

Tameka and her mom put their arms around each other and pose for the picture. Then the three of them gather around to see how it turned out. There they are: Tameka and Mom, looking almost like smiling twins in their graduation gowns and caps.

"A college graduate and an elementary-school graduate, in the same family and in the same week," Dad says. "Now, that's something I'm really proud of. I'll have to email this picture to everyone we know."

Mom says, "Wow, it's really happening, isn't it? I mean, I went back to school after all that time off, and now I'm done! Thanks for supporting me through it all, you two." She gives them both a quick hug. Then she turns to her daughter, saying, "Now that we know how these gowns fit, I'm going to shorten the hem on yours. We want you looking fine when you walk across that stage on Friday."

Tameka's stomach feels like it's doing flips. "Tell her," she thinks. "Just tell her!" But Tameka can't find the words to say how scared she is about going up on stage with the rest of her class. Or how the thought of starting middle school next year keeps her awake at night.

"How can I tell her I'm afraid," Tameka thinks, "when Mom's getting her college degree—with *honors*—and did it all while working a part-time job? Mom is so brave, and she never stops reaching for her goals. She wouldn't let a few butterflies get in her way. How come I'm not more like her?"

Although Tameka has the *Adult Role Models* asset, she has doubts about herself and isn't sure what to do.

Think about your own life. Are there adults in your family you look up to and want to be like? What about other grown-ups you know?

If **YES**, keep reading to learn ways to make this asset even stronger.

If **NO**, keep reading to learn ways to add this asset to your life.

You can also use these ideas to help add this asset for other people—like your friends, family members, neighbors, and kids at school.

> ## Facts!
>
> **Kids with the *Adult Role Models* asset:**
>
> ✔ **are better readers**
>
> ✔ **are less *aggressive* (pushy and violent)**
>
> ✔ **have higher hopes for their own future**

ways to Add This Asset

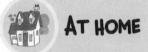 **AT HOME**

Think About Your Family Role Models. Which adults in your family do you admire most? Try to think of at least three. What about your parents? Grandparents? Aunts and uncles? Foster parents or guardians? Older siblings or cousins? Now think of at least one quality you appreciate about each person. *Examples:* "My mom keeps her sense of humor, even when times are tough." "My grandpa is kind to everyone." "My big sister works really hard at being a good basketball player." "My stepdad can fix anything." You might write about this person in your journal. Better yet, send him or her a note or an email saying, "I think you're great because. . . ."

6 Ways to Be a Good Role Model

It's not just grown-ups who are role models. Younger kids look up to older kids—like you. They watch you and copy what you say and do. Here's how to be a good role model for them:

1. Think about what you say in front of them.

2. Think about how you act in front of them.

3. Show that you respect yourself and others.

4. Spend time with them. Help them to know that they matter.

5. Have healthy habits. Eat good food. Exercise. Keep yourself neat and clean.

6. Be a reader. If little kids see you reading, they'll want to do it, too.

(Whew! Being a good role model is a big responsibility!)

Name More of Your Role Models. When kids are asked to name their role models, they often name TV stars, sports figures, rappers, singers, models, and actors. These people have fame and fortune, but are they really *role models*? A role model is someone who acts in positive, responsible ways. Some rich and famous people act the exact opposite! Can you think of three celebrities who *truly* fit the definition? Write down their names. *Then . . .*

Give Them the "Sniff Test." For each celebrity you named, ask yourself: "Is this someone who lives a clean and healthy life? Does the person make good decisions? Is he or she helping others? Is the person setting a good example?" Some celebrities are real stinkers. If that's true for the names on your list, try to come up with different role models.

TIP: Role models don't have to be famous or rich. They can be your neighbors, your teachers, or someone you learned about in school. They don't even have to be real people. Is there a character you admire in a book you read? What about a character on a TV show?

Know That Even Role Models Make Mistakes. Nobody's perfect—not even the role models that millions of people look up to. World leaders, heroes, and peacemakers make mistakes, just like the rest of us. Talk with a family adult about a famous role model who made a mistake, big or small. Did that person admit the error and apologize? What did the person learn from the mistake? How did he or she try to make things right?

Make a Role Model Collage. First, think of people you admire. For family members, ask for their pictures, or take pictures with a disposable camera, or make your own drawings. For celebrity role models, look for their pictures in magazines, the newspaper, or online. Glue the images on a piece of posterboard or construction paper. Next, cut out words from magazines or newspapers that say what you admire about each person. These might be words like *success*, *giving*, *kindness*, *honor*, *courage*, *inspiration*, *wise*, *goals*, *strong*, and *respect*. Glue the words near the images. Finally, hang your collage on a bulletin board or your wall so it can inspire you every day. Or keep it in your journal, where you can look at it in private.

 ## AT SCHOOL

★ Think of a national or world figure you see as a role model. Spend time in your school's library or media center learning more about the person. Ask the librarian to help you find books, articles,

> **TIP:** Maybe this could be an independent study project—something you share with your classroom teacher or even your whole class.

or videos. Write down reasons why the person is a good role model.

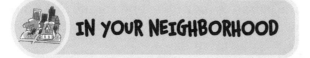 ## IN YOUR NEIGHBORHOOD

★ Which of your neighbors are good role models? What about the mom who waits for the school bus with the little kids every morning? Or the dad who volunteers as a softball coach at the park? Or the teenagers who trick-or-treat for UNICEF each Halloween? Or the family with the McGruff House sign on their window? Ask your parents or other family adults to tell you about neighbors they admire.

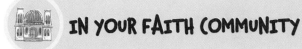

IN YOUR FAITH COMMUNITY

★ Talk with your religious leaders about role models. Who do they admire and why? Look for role models in your faith community. Are there adults you respect and admire? How can you get to know them better?

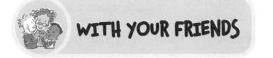

WITH YOUR FRIENDS

★ In one national survey of kids ages 10–13, almost half of them said they had *no* role models. Everyone needs at least one person to look up to and admire. Ask your friends who their role models are. If someone says "No one," talk more about this. Maybe you could suggest a role model or two for your friend to consider. Or tell your friend which role models you have chosen and why.

Possible Role Models

✓ Madeleine Albright
64 US Secretary of
State (Jan. 23, 1997–Jan.
16, 2001)

✓ Yo-Yo Ma
Cellist

✓ Adam Werbach
Former
Sierra Club
President

Start Adding!

Pick at least ONE idea you've read here and give it a try. Then think about or write about what happened. Will you try another way to find adults who are good role models for you?

After her dad goes to email the photo, Tameka decides to talk to her mom about what's on her mind.

Back to Tameka's Story

"Mom," Tameka asks, "are you nervous about going up on stage to get your diploma?"

"Sure, a little. Why? Are you?"

"Yep, I am. I don't think I can do it, Mom. I *hate* having to do stuff in front of people! Just thinking about it right now is making my stomach jump around."

Her mom puts her hands on Tameka's shoulders and looks into her eyes. "Everybody gets nervous."

"Not you."

"Yes, me!"

"But, Mom, you're like Superwoman or something. You work at a job and you just put yourself through college and you also find time for Dad and me. I'm, like, a total loser compared to you."

"Tameka, don't talk that way! I'm really proud of you—and so is your dad. You study so hard, and you have a bright future ahead of you. You can do anything you set your mind to."

Tameka looks away. "I don't know if I can. I'm just not that sure of myself."

"You know, I'm not always so sure of myself either," her mom answers. "But my mom always said I could do anything. And I believed her—because you know Grandma, she's a strong woman."

"I know," Tameka answers. "I look up to her a lot."

"And your dad helped me be more confident, too," her mom continues. "Every time he said 'I believe in you,' it helped me."

"Yeah, Dad's pretty awesome. But I still feel, I don't know, *stressed*. Like I don't know if I can do it."

"Well, I'm pretty lucky, because I've had one extra thing that gives me confidence and keeps me motivated to achieve my goals. And you know what that one thing is?" She pauses, then looks at Tameka and says, "*You*."

"Me? Really?" Tameka asks.

"Yeah, really. You help me be strong and reach for better things. Thanks to you and, of course, Dad, I'm wearing this gown today."

"So, you're saying *I'm* kind of a role model for *you*?" Tameka asks in surprise.

"That's exactly what I'm saying!" her mom answers with a smile.

Positive Peer Influence

ALVERO'S STORY

The school bus is headed for the last stop of the morning. Alvero tenses as the brakes squeal to a loud halt.

"Here he comes!" says Tanner eagerly as Bobby climbs up the bus steps. "Watch this, Alv."

As Bobby walks to the back of the bus, Tanner sticks out his leg and says, "Don't trip." Bobby falls over, spilling his notebooks and folders. Many of the kids laugh, but not Alvero.

Tanner turns to Alvero and says, "Dude, lighten up, it's *funny*."

As Bobby picks up his dirtied papers, the bus driver calls out, "C'mon, Bobby, take a seat."

Tanner chimes in with, "Yeah, Bobby the Baby better take his seat before he starts *cwy-ing*."

More kids laugh this time, making Alvero wince.

"Okay, now," says the bus driver. "Let's all give him a break."

Alvero turns away from Tanner and peers out the window, watching the buildings pass by. When he's sure Tanner isn't looking, he sneaks a peek back at Bobby. Bobby is sitting alone in the farthest seat back, looking like he doesn't have a friend in the world.

"How long is this going to keep up?" Alvero wonders. "Why does Tanner have to act this way every single day?"

Alvero and Bobby don't have the *Positive Peer Influence* asset.

Think about your own life. Do your close friends behave in positive, responsible ways? Are they a good influence on you? Do they help you to do and be your best?

If **YES,** keep reading to learn ways to make this asset even stronger.

If **NO,** keep reading to learn ways to add this asset to your life.

You can also use these ideas to help add this asset for other people—like your friends, family members, neighbors, and kids at school.

Facts!

Kids with the *Positive Peer* Influence asset:

✓ care more about school

✓ stay away from cigarettes, alcohol, and other drugs

✓ get along better with others and feel more connected to other people

ways to Add This Asset

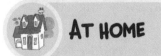 **AT HOME**

Ask Yourself Who Your Friends Are. Write down the names of all of your friends—people at school, in your neighborhood, in your faith community, and in any

programs, clubs, or activities you go to. Now think carefully about each person. What words would you use to describe him or her? Write those words by each person's name.

> **TiP:** Do this in your at-home journal so it's private. You don't want other people to see your list or feelings might get hurt.

Ask Yourself Who You Are with Your Friends. Can you just be yourself? Or do you put on an act to please certain people? Some of your friends may bring out the best in you, while others may not. Which friends help you feel really good about yourself, and why? Write your thoughts in your journal. You can also talk with a family adult about the ups and downs of your friendships.

Get a Grown-up's Opinion. Ask the adults in your family what they think of your friends. Do they seem to be a good influence on you? Why or why not?

TiP: If your parents want to get to know your friends, they're not being nosy. They're showing that they care.

BONUS TiP: Some adults are quick to judge kids based on how they look. Once parents get to know kids, clothes or hair don't matter as much.

SUPER BONUS TiP: If your parents want to get to know your friends' parents, that's great! No matter whose home you're at, adults will be watching out for you.

SUPER DOOPER BONUS TiP: See if you can get to know your friends' parents. It's good to have other caring adults in your life.

Get Real About Your Friends. What if thinking about your friends, writing in your journal, and talking with adults have made you wonder about some of your friendships? You have choices. You can talk with your friends about ways to make your friendships better and stronger. You can make new friends. Or you can start spending *less* time with people who don't act like true friends (see the list on page 65) and *more* time with those who do.

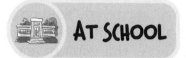

AT SCHOOL

★ You spend more of your awake time at school than you do anywhere else. Many of your friends are probably kids you know at school. Do they take school seriously? Are they good students? Do they treat teachers with respect? Are they nice to other kids? These are the kinds of friends you want—not kids who goof off, make trouble, or bully others. What if this means you need to make new friends? It won't be easy, but it's worth it. You might talk with a teacher you like and trust about how to start.

★ Is your school full of cliques? Maybe you're in one. Or maybe you're dying to get into one. Even though cliques are a fact of life, you don't have to let them run your life. Look around for other kids who aren't in cliques. They might be a lot more interesting and fun than kids who are.

★ Want to know a fast way to make a new friend? Get to know the new kid at school. Smile, say hi, and offer to show him or her around.

IN YOUR NEIGHBORHOOD

★ After-school activities and community programs are great places to make friends. Find out what your school offers. With a family adult, check out the choices in your neighborhood or community. Look around for programs that will not only give you something to do, but will also help make you a better person. That's how you'll find other positive, responsible people to hang out with.

IN YOUR FAITH COMMUNITY

★ Your faith community is a great place to make friends who share your values. It's also a great place to talk about the *Positive Peer Influence* asset with other kids and caring adults. Maybe you can do this in your religion class, or in your youth group. Start a conversation about what makes a good friend—or a bad influence.

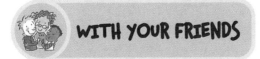

WITH YOUR FRIENDS

★ Try to be a good influence on your friends. If they behave in negative ways or take foolish risks, don't just go along. Tell them how you feel. Try to talk them into making better choices. If a friend is about to do something really dumb or dangerous, tell an adult right away. That's not being a snitch—it's being a real friend.

A message for you

Right now, and for the rest of your life, people will pressure you to "join the crowd." We all want to fit in and be liked. But whenever you hear someone say, "Come on—everyone is doing it!" step back and think for yourself. Especially if it's something that seems fishy or risky. For example, everyone is *not* cheating on tests. Everyone is *not* using cigarettes, alcohol, or other drugs. Everyone is *not* breaking the rules. Don't fall for the "everyone" line. If you have trouble figuring out what's right for you, talk with an adult you trust.

★ With your friends, read the "10 Signs of a True Friend" list below. Do you fit the description of a true friend? Do they? Be honest with each other. What can each of you do to be a better friend, starting today?

10 Signs of a True Friend

A true friend is someone who:

1. respects you

2. cares about you

3. listens to you

4. sticks up for you

5. helps you when you need help

6. encourages you to make good choices

7. doesn't put you down

8. doesn't talk behind your back

9. tells you the truth

10. laughs at your jokes (even your worst ones)

Start Adding!

Pick at least ONE idea you've read here and give it a try. Then think about or write about what happened. Will you try another way to find friends who help you do and be your best?

Back to
Alvero's
Story

As the kids file off the bus and head into school, Alvero falls behind, lost in thought. Tanner runs ahead, saying, "Catch you later, Alv! I'm going to see if Bobby the Baby has anything for me in his lunch box today."

Although Alvero is angry about how Bobby is being treated, he stays silent. "Tanner's my best buddy," he thinks. "I can't tell him to back off."

Right then, Julia, the girl Alvero has a crush on, doubles back and walks toward him. His heart skips a beat. "Nice *friend* you've got there," she says, sounding sarcastic. She turns away, leaving Alvero in the dust.

"That's just great," Alvero mutters. "Can this day get any worse?" Then he makes a decision he's been putting off for ages.

He finds Tanner at the lockers and blurts out, "Tanner, I've got something to say to you."

Tanner and a bunch of other kids look at him expectantly. Alvero knows he's taking a big risk, but he doesn't feel he has a choice anymore. It's time to stand up for what he believes in—even if everyone turns on him.

He gathers his courage and says, "Enough is enough, Tanner. I'm tired of the way you're treating Bobby. No one deserves to get picked on day after day. It's not cool, it's not fair, and it's not funny."

"Are you guys hearing this?" says Tanner, grinning.

But no one else is smiling. They're waiting to see what happens next.

Noticing this, Alvero decides to say something else. "I'm telling you right now, if we're going to stay friends, you've got to chill out about Bobby."

Tanner smirks and starts to turn away—but then he stops. "Okay, okay, when you put it that way. . . ." He reaches out his hand for Alvero to shake. "Peace?"

"Yeah," says Alvero. "Peace."

High Expectations

What it means: Your parents and teachers expect you to do your best at school and in other activities.

Kira's Story

Kira pushes her books and papers off of her desk and onto her bedroom floor. *CRASH!* They fall in a heap by the bedroom door, where her dad suddenly appears.

"What was that?" he asks, out of breath from running up the stairs. Then he spies the mess. "Ah," he says. "Must be another math test."

"Yeah," Kira replies in tears. "And I'm going to flunk!"

Her dad bends over and picks up the textbook that Kira has grown to hate. "This fat book *would* make a nice doorstop," he says with a wry smile. "But I think you might need it for more important things—like math."

Kira only cries harder.

"That was a joke," her dad adds, picking up papers, pencils, and folders.

"I can't stand pre-Algebra, Dad! I could study all night and still get a bad grade."

"Kira, I expect more from you than this," her dad replies softly.

"That's what I mean!" she wails. "I can't do it, and I'm letting everyone down!"

Before her dad can say another word, Kira runs past him out of the room and down the stairs.

> **Kira is worried and confused about the *High Expectations* asset.**

Facts!

Kids with the *High Expectations* asset:

✔ want to succeed in school

✔ get better grades in school

✔ expect more of themselves

Think about your own life. Do your parents and teachers expect you to do your best at school? What about other activities?

If **YES**, keep reading to learn ways to make this asset even stronger.

If **NO**, keep reading to learn ways to add this asset to your life.

You can also use these ideas to help add this asset for other people—like your friends, family members, neighbors, and kids at school.

ways to Add This Asset

AT HOME

Talk, Talk, Talk. Do you know what your parents or other important adults in your life *really* expect of you? Sometimes kids get confused about their parents' expectations, thinking they're supposed to bring home top grades or be the star goalie. But what many parents want is for their kids to *try THEIR best*, not always *be THE best*. Have you talked to the grown-ups in your family about this? What are their expectations for you? Are they realistic . . . or too high?

Keep Your Own Expectations High Yet Reachable. You want to s-t-r-e-t-c-h to reach them, but they shouldn't be out of reach. Talk about your expectations with the adults in your life. Ask for their help and guidance.

> **TiP:** What if someone says, "You'll never do that," or "Forget about that"? Find someone else to talk to—someone who will support and encourage you.

Let Yourself Make Mistakes. You won't get everything right on the first try—and sometimes not on the second or third try, either. When you make a mistake, don't be hard on yourself. Try to do better next time.

5 Facts About Mistakes

1. Everyone makes mistakes.

2. Mistakes prove that you're trying.

3. Mistakes are a chance to get it right the next time.

4. Mistakes are great teachers. You can learn a lot from them.

5. Mistakes aren't failures. They're steps on the road to success.

Forget About Being Perfect. Nobody's perfect! If you try to be perfect, you'll get stuck. You'll be afraid of taking risks or trying anything new. Instead, give yourself permission to make at least three mistakes a day. Then go ahead and make them.

Start a Quotes Collection. Look in books or magazines for quotations that will inspire you to do and be your best. Write them in your notebook or journal. If there's a quote you like a lot, tape it to your mirror where you'll see it every day. Here's one to start with: "High expectations are the key to everything"—Sam Walton. (*P.S.* Sam Walton was the founder of Wal-Mart.)

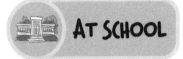

AT SCHOOL

★ Tell your teachers what you want to accomplish in school. Ask for their help and support. This will encourage them to set high expectations for you—and to pay more attention to how you're doing.

IN YOUR NEIGHBORHOOD

★ Have high expectations for younger kids in your neighborhood. Ask them how they're doing in school. Set a good example for them by how you act when you're around them.

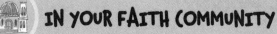

IN YOUR FAITH COMMUNITY

★ What does your faith community expect of you and other kids your age? What does your religion or your cultural traditions say about how you should behave and what goals you should reach for? Talk about these questions with your friends, your religion class, and your youth group.

WITH YOUR FRIENDS

★ Have high expectations for each other. Encourage each other to do well at school. Show up at each other's games, performances, or practices and cheer.

★ If a friend does something risky or dangerous, don't just ignore it. Speak up. You can say, "Hey, watch out! I care about you, and I don't want you to get hurt." Let your friend know that you expect more of him or her.

Start Adding!

Pick at least ONE idea you've read here and give it a try. Then think about or write about what happened. Will you try another way to make sure there are people in your life who expect the best from you?

Back to
Kira's
Story
Kira throws herself facedown on the family room couch, where she cries into a pillow.

"Hey, drama queen," says her stepbrother, Jay. "Why don't you use a tissue?"

Kira throws the pillow at him and screams, "Shut up! Leave me alone!"

"Whoa, whoa, whoa," says her dad, entering the room. "Kira, you need to calm down so we can talk."

"I'm outta here," says Jay. "I'm sick of her crying fits."

Kira's dad pulls a chair next to the couch and sits down. "All right, Kira, I'd like you to tell me why you ran out of your room. And why you're crying."

Her words come out in a rush. "Because you expect me to get all A's and I can't do it in math, and my teacher always piles on the homework, and then every time we have a test I don't know what I'm doing, and I just keep reading the questions over and over without knowing the answers, and . . . and . . . ."

"Slow down a minute," he says, "and take a deep breath. I never said I expect straight A's. And I know you're having trouble in math, but—"

"But you and Mom are happy when I get A's," Kira interrupts, "and that means you won't be happy if I don't!"

Her dad sighs. "We need to get something straight right now. I'm happy with you because of *who you are*, not because of the grades you get—although I *am* pleased that you study hard and do well. And I think I can speak for Mom when I say that she feels the same way."

"Well, for sure you don't expect me to *flunk*," Kira says stubbornly.

"Of course we don't," her dad replies. "And there are ways to make sure you won't. I'll help, and so will Mom. And believe it or not, Jay knows a lot about math. He can help you, too."

"Jay would help *me*? That's a good one, Dad!"

"I'm serious! He told me last night that he wishes you'd just come and ask once in a while."

"Really?" Kira sits up and wipes her eyes.

"Really," Dad answers. "And you and I can talk to your teacher to see if you need some extra help from a tutor. The important thing is to give it your best shot. Which *doesn't* mean shooting your book across the desk and onto the floor."

Kira laughs and hugs her dad. "I love you," she says. "Let's go see if Jay can help me get ready for this test—and the sooner the better!"

A NOTE TO GROWN-UPS

Ongoing research by Search Institute, a nonprofit organization based in Minneapolis, Minnesota, shows that young people who succeed have specific assets in their lives—**Developmental Assets** including family support, a caring neighborhood, integrity, resistance skills, self-esteem, and a sense of purpose. This book, along with the other seven books in the **Adding Assets Series for Kids**, empowers young people ages 8–12 to build their own Developmental Assets.

But it's very important to acknowledge that building assets for and with young people is primarily an *adult* responsibility. What kids need most in their lives are grown-ups—parents and other relatives, teachers, school administrators, neighbors, youth leaders, religious leaders, community members, policy makers, advocates, and more—who care about them as individuals. They need adults who care enough to learn their names, to show interest in their lives, to listen when they talk, to provide them with opportunities to realize their potential, to teach them well, to give them sound advice, to serve as good examples, to guide them, to inspire them, to support them when they stumble, and to shield them from harm—as much as is humanly possible these days.

This book focuses on six of the 40 Developmental Assets identified by Search Institute. These are **External Assets**—positive experiences kids receive from the world around them. The six external assets described here are called the **Boundaries and Expectations Assets**.

Boundaries guide kids to make positive choices. Children are more likely to thrive when they have clear, consistent, age-appropriate rules about how to behave, and clear, consistent, reasonable consequences for breaking those rules. They need rules and consequences in all areas of their lives, which is why there are three boundaries assets: Family, School, and Neighborhood.

Children are also guided by how other people behave. They imitate adults and are strongly influenced by their peers. That's why this asset category also includes Adult Role Models and Positive Peer Influence.

Finally, children need encouragement from the adults in their lives. They need parents, teachers, and others to have High Expectations of them—the sixth asset in this category. High expectations can bring out the best in a child, as long as they're not so high that the child can't ever hope to reach them. Expectations should be realistic and often revamped to keep up with our children's changing abilities, talents, and experiences.

A list of all 40 Developmental Assets for middle childhood, with definitions, follows. If you want to know more about the assets, some of the resources listed on pages 86–87 will help you. Or you can visit the Search Institute Web site at *www.search-institute.org*.

Thank you for caring enough about kids to make this book available to the young person or persons in your life. We'd love to hear your success stories, and we welcome your suggestions for adding assets to kids' lives—or improving future editions of this book.

Pamela Espeland and Elizabeth Verdick
Free Spirit Publishing Inc.
217 Fifth Avenue North, Suite 200
Minneapolis, MN 55401-1299
help4kids@freespirit.com

The 40 Developmental Assets for Middle Childhood

EXTERNAL ASSETS

SUPPORT

1. **Family support**—Family life provides high levels of love and support.
2. **Positive family communication**—Parent(s) and child communicate positively. Child feels comfortable seeking advice and counsel from parent(s).
3. **Other adult relationships**—Child receives support from adults other than her or his parent(s).
4. **Caring neighborhood**—Child experiences caring neighbors.
5. **Caring school climate**—Relationships with teachers and peers provide a caring, encouraging school environment.
6. **Parent involvement in schooling**—Parent(s) are actively involved in helping the child succeed in school.

EMPOWERMENT

7. **Community values children**—Child feels valued and appreciated by adults in the community.
8. **Children as resources**—Child is included in decisions at home and in the community.
9. **Service to others**—Child has opportunities to help others in the community.
10. **Safety**—Child feels safe at home, at school, and in her or his neighborhood.

BOUNDARIES AND EXPECTATIONS

11. **Family boundaries**—Family has clear and consistent rules and consequences and monitors the child's whereabouts.
12. **School boundaries**—School provides clear rules and consequences.
13. **Neighborhood boundaries**—Neighbors take responsibility for monitoring the child's behavior.
14. **Adult role models**—Parents(s) and other adults in the child's family, as well as nonfamily adults, model positive, responsible behavior.
15. **Positive peer influence**—Child's closest friends model positive, responsible behavior.
16. **High expectations**—Parent(s) and teachers expect the child to do her or his best at school and in other activities.

CONSTRUCTIVE USE OF TIME

17. **Creative activities**—Child participates in music, art, drama, or creative writing two or more times per week.
18. **Child programs**—Child participates two or more times per week in cocurricular school activities or structured community programs for children.
19. **Religious community**—Child attends religious programs or services one or more times per week.
20. **Time at home**—Child spends some time most days both in high-quality interaction with parent(s) and doing things at home other than watching TV or playing video games.

COMMITMENT TO LEARNING

1. **Achievement motivation**—Child is motivated and strives to do well in school.
2. **Learning engagement**—Child is responsive, attentive, and actively engaged in learning at school and enjoys participating in learning activities outside of school.
3. **Homework**—Child usually hands in homework on time.
4. **Bonding to adults at school**—Child cares about teachers and other adults at school.
5. **Reading for pleasure**—Child enjoys and engages in reading for fun most days of the week.

POSITIVE VALUES

6. **Caring**—Parent(s) tell the child it is important to help other people.
7. **Equality and social justice**—Parent(s) tell the child it is important to speak up for equal rights for all people.
8. **Integrity**—Parent(s) tell the child it is important to stand up for one's beliefs.
9. **Honesty**—Parent(s) tell the child it is important to tell the truth.
10. **Responsibility**—Parent(s) tell the child it is important to accept personal responsibility for behavior.
11. **Healthy lifestyle**—Parent(s) tell the child it is important to have good health habits and an understanding of healthy sexuality.

SOCIAL COMPETENCIES

12. **Planning and decision making**—Child thinks about decisions and is usually happy with the results of her or his decisions.
13. **Interpersonal competence**—Child cares about and is affected by other people's feelings, enjoys making friends, and, when frustrated or angry, tries to calm herself or himself.
14. **Cultural competence**—Child knows and is comfortable with people of different racial, ethnic, and cultural backgrounds and with her or his own cultural identity.
15. **Resistance skills**—Child can stay away from people who are likely to get her or him in trouble and is able to say no to doing wrong or dangerous things.
16. **Peaceful conflict resolution**—Child attempts to resolve conflict nonviolently.

POSITIVE IDENTITY

17. **Personal power**—Child feels he or she has some influence over things that happen in her or his life.
18. **Self-esteem**—Child likes and is proud to be the person he or she is.
19. **Sense of purpose**—Child sometimes thinks about what life means and whether there is a purpose for her or his life.
20. **Positive view of personal future**—Child is optimistic about her or his personal future.

Helpful Resources

Books

The Kid's Guide to Service Projects by Barbara A. Lewis (Minneapolis: Free Spirit Publishing, 1995). Describes hundreds of ways to make a difference, from simple things you can do on your own to projects that might involve your whole community. Topics include animals, crime fighting, the environment, friendship, hunger, literacy, politics and government, and transportation.

Reaching Your Goals by Robin Landew Silverman (New York: Franklin Watts, 2004). To turn a wish into a goal takes creative thinking and organized planning skills. This book shows how to make a plan and see it through to the end.

Think for Yourself: A Kid's Guide to Solving Life's Dilemmas and Other Sticky Problems by Cynthia MacGregor (Toronto: Lobster Press, 2003). Daily problems are broken down into easy-to-follow categories: friends, family, grown-ups, and everyday situations. Real-life examples and choices for solutions reinforce the importance of thinking things through and doing what's best for you.

What Do You Stand For? For Kids by Barbara A. Lewis (Minneapolis: Free Spirit Publishing, 1999). Being your best means knowing what it takes to be a caring, cooperative, honest person. This book is full of activities, advice, and inspiring true stories.

84

Who Knew? 25 Quizzes to Help You Find Your Secret by Beth Mayall (New York: Scholastic, Inc., 2001). What makes you special and unique? Takes these quizzes and uncover your one-of-a-kind qualities and hidden strengths. Some are serious, some are silly, and all tell you something you might not already know about yourself.

Web sites

Kids Meeting Kids
www.kidsmeetingkids.org
This Web site connects young people from different countries and cultures to make this a better and safer world. Sign on to learn how you can help bring peace and fairness to all kids.

National Youth Leadership Council (NYLC)
www.nylc.org
The NYLC brings kids, educators, and community leaders together to make sure that kids are seen, heard, and actively involved in community organizations and decision making.

Youth as Resources
www.yar.org
Kids really can make a difference. YAR supports youth-led service projects, from juvenile justice to public housing and any issue that motivates kids to make our world a better place. Find a YAR program near you, or start your own.

Youth Service America
www.servenet.org
A helpful national resource to connect to organizations and service projects in your area. Type in your ZIP code, skills, and interests to find the best service experience for you.

FOR ADULTS

Books

Building Assets Is Elementary: Group Activities for Helping Kids Ages 8–12 Succeed by Search Institute (Minneapolis: Search Institute, 2004). Promoting creativity, time-management skills, kindness, manners, and more, this flexible activity book includes over 50 easy-to-use group exercises for the classroom or youth group.

How to Parent So Children Will Learn by Sylvia B. Rimm, Ph.D. (Three Rivers, MI: Three Rivers Press, 1997). Advice on setting limits, selecting appropriate rewards and punishments, decreasing arguments and power struggles, encouraging appropriate independence, guiding children toward good study habits, helping them improve their test-taking skills, and much more.

What Kids Need to Succeed: Proven, Practical Ways to Raise Good Kids by Peter L. Benson, Ph.D., Judy Galbraith, M.A., and Pamela Espeland (Minneapolis: Free Spirit Publishing, 1994). More than 900 specific, concrete suggestions help adults help children build Developmental Assets at home, at school, and in the community.

What Young Children Need to Succeed: Working Together to Build Assets from Birth to Age 11 by Jolene L. Roehlkepartain and Nancy Leffert, Ph.D. (Minneapolis: Free Spirit Publishing, 2000). Hundreds of practical, concrete ideas help adults build Developmental Assets for children in four different age groups: birth to 12 months, ages 1–2, 3–5, and 6–11. Includes inspiring true stories from across the United States.

Web sites

Connect for Kids
www.connectforkids.org
Tips, articles, resources, volunteer opportunities, and more for adults who want to improve the lives of children in their community and beyond. Includes the complete text of Richard Louv's book *101 Things You Can Do for Our Children's Future*.

The Giraffe Project
www.giraffe.org
The Giraffe Project works to inspire K–12 students to be courageous, active citizens. Their site includes helpful resources and extraordinary stories about heroes of all ages who are willing to stick out their necks to help others.

National Mentoring Partnership
www.mentoring.org
The organization provides connections, training, resources, and advice to introduce and support mentoring partnerships. The site is a wealth of information about becoming and finding a mentor.

Search Institute
www.search-institute.org
Through dynamic research and analysis, this independent nonprofit organization works to promote healthy, active, and content youth and communities.

Index

About the Authors

Both Pamela Espeland and Elizabeth Verdick have written many books for children and teens.

Pamela is the coauthor (with Peter L. Benson and Judy Galbraith) of *What Kids Need to Succeed* and *What Teens Need to Succeed* and the author of *Succeed Every Day*, all based on Search Institute's concept of the 40 Developmental Assets. She is the author of *Life Lists for Teens* and the coauthor (with Gershen Kaufman and Lev Raphael) of *Stick Up for Yourself!*

Elizabeth is a children's book writer and editor. She is the author of *Teeth Are Not for Biting, Words Are Not for Hurting*, and *Feet Are Not for Kicking* and coauthor (with Marjorie Lisovskis) of *How to Take the GRRRR Out of Anger* and (with Trevor Romain) of *Stress Can Really Get on Your Nerves* and *True or False? Tests Stink!*

Pamela and Elizabeth first worked together on *Making Every Day Count*. They live in Minnesota with their families and pets.

More Titles in the Adding Assets Series for Kids

By Pamela Espeland and Elizabeth Verdick. Each book is for ages 8–12. *Each $9.95; softcover; two-color illust., 5⅛" x 7".*

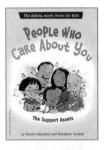

People Who Care About You

Kids learn how to build the six Support Assets: Family Support, Positive Family Communication, Other Adult Relationships, Caring Neighborhood, Caring School Climate, and Parent Involvement in Schooling. Stories, tips, and ideas bring them closer to their families and strengthen other important relationships in their lives. *96 pp.*

Helping Out and Staying Safe

Kids learn how to build the four Empowerment Assets: Community Values Children, Children as Resources, Service to Others, and Safety. Stories, tips, and ideas guide them to play useful roles at home and in the community, help others, and feel safer at home, at school, and in their neighborhood. *80 pp.*

Smart Ways to Spend Your Time

Kids learn how to build the four Constructive Use of Time Assets: Creative Activities, Child Programs, Religious Community, and Time at Home. Stories, tips, and ideas promote healthy, constructive, relationship-strengthening interests and activities. *96 pp.*